Silly Signs

Silly Signs

From the farcical to the downright ridiculous

ARCTURUS

ARCTURUS

This edition published in 2012 by Arcturus Publishing Limited
26/27 Bickels Yard, 151–153 Bermondsey Street,
London SE1 3HA

ISBN: 978-1-84858-417-4
AD002025EN

Printed in China

Most signs are boring (especially the sign for Boring, Oregon). Efficient and simple, they give their information with a minimum of fuss. So isn't it nice when you see a sign that bucks the trend? In this collection of silly signs you'll come across all sorts of weird and wonderful examples that will put a smile on your face – even if it's one of those thinly veiled threats to KEEP OUT OR DIE! Some of these signs have been created with the intention of making us laugh, others are funny because they are NOT supposed to be funny, like the sign for a school, misspelt 'Shcool', or the burial site notice that warns 'No Exit'. Whatever you do in life, read the signs – but beware of taking them too literally.

At the National Institute for Paranormal Research,
local kids are becoming a nuisance.

Honestly, if you need this sign to tell you how to sit on a toilet, you probably shouldn't be going on your own.

Selling like hot cakes.

After depositing his shiny new penny,
Philip regretted using his wish so rashly.

Dad, why are you wearing a penguin costume?

His hamburgers are the worst you'll ever taste,
but at least Honest Al tells it like it is.

A one-way route with no get-out clause.
Proceed with caution.

Basically, you're screwed.

No. That's just nonsense that is.

Home from home.

**Bill's career as a weather forecaster
was not going entirely to plan.**

Janette began to wish she'd done as she was told
and gone when they parked the coach.

The curved yellow fruit are located in the sweet and relatively healthy edible aisle next to the round, kind of amber-coloured, pimply-skinned objects and the green, or perhaps red, slightly smaller ... oh, I give up.

'You'll never take me alive!'
Tim the seagull's challenging behaviour reaches new
heights as his authority-issues come to the fore.

Now you know you've reached the middle of nowhere.

If you happen to be visiting from 1876,
lol means 'laugh out loud' in textspeak.

This sign isn't half as funny in English.

A lonely, cold and agonizing death, or a nice hot chocolate at the lodge. The choice is yours.

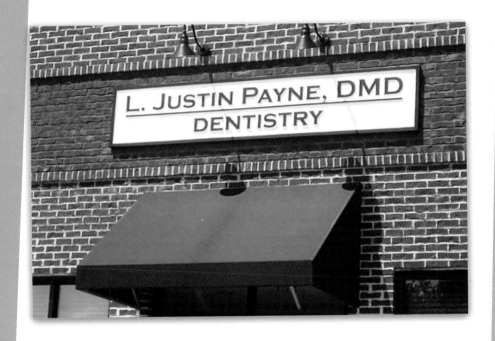

Whoever heard of a dentist with a sense of humour?

Dumb …

… and dumber.

Whoever thought of keeping alligators at the bottom of this incredibly steep hill is either an evil madman, or a comedy genius.

Damn it, my quest for a black eggs shop
will have to wait until another day.

Do you take credit cards?

So sayeth the Lord.

Many a fickle fellow has arrived at this crossroads.

It's a lot cheaper than flowers.

Don't you just love places where Big Brother gives you a choice?

See how how much nicer it sounds when you say please?

The cunning thing about this sign is that you have
to slow down to read it all.

Hey! That's no way to attach a tow bar!

From the sublime ...

… to the ridiculous!

After 15 minutes of trying to follow airport directions, Jane realized she no longer knew whether she was coming or going.

Sign of the times.

. . . underwater.

Or, if you're really worried, just sit on them.

They may look cute, but those penguins will steal your
wheels faster than you can say, 'Happy Feet'.

This Thai sign offers sympathy, but not sense.

The road less travelled.

Rest assured that, if you do have permission,
trespassing is absolutely fine.

TANAH PERSENDIRIAN
DILARANG MASUK
私人重地禁止進入
PRIVATE PROPERTY
NO TRESPASSING

But there are some trespassing signs you just obey.

Bargain! I'd charge far more than that.

At the end of a lonely three years spent attempting to hack
the county's road sign network, James smiled the smile
of a man who knows every second was worth it.

49

Try for an earlier appointment.

The age-old battle of Good versus Google.

At Clever Dick's Fish Bar, you get what you pay for.

Do you know this supermarket?
Perhaps you know where it is now?
If so, we'd like to hear from you.

But sometimes the car comes off worse!

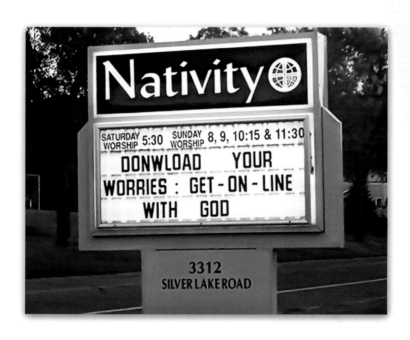

**Just don't expect faster broadband –
he's good, but not THAT good.**

Jim the mechanic thought he'd been terribly witty until customers started taking him literally.

Some days you go in the sea and it just makes you tingle all over.

The Forest Rangers' annual party ended in predictable hilarity.

The drains at this service station clearly aren't up to much.

Not just any old jumping walrus... he's the sensitive one with the clutch bag and stick-on eyelashes.

A fresh take on the hard luck story.

Brain not engaged.

No Littering
Violators will be fine
此處不准倒垃圾
違者嚴罰

That's reassuring.

The residents of Nagasaki become increasingly
uncomfortable as the haemorrhoid epidemic takes hold.
Medics blame a regional prune shortage.

Beware falling spacemen.

A-Team approaching.

... for crimes against fashion?

What part of 'Please DO <u>NOT</u>' don't you understand?

… NO breathing.

'… I'm not lost.'

The minister likes his little jokes …

Verse from the Old Testament?

'Mummy, can we go home now?' Even on her 46th crossing, Sue still found the experience strangely invigorating.

Looks like someone should have shtayed in school.

You've obviously never tried to push start a Buick.

Lost in translation?

Clint Eastwood's parking space.

If you were thinking of parking your vehicle in a toilet, this doesn't look like the one you'd choose.

Determined to improve his Spanish,
Colin the penguin practises. Hard.

Faced with a rocketing number of injury claims,
Professor Dumbledore decided to tackle the matter head on.

Perfect as part of a protein-packed mythical beast omelette.

Sue soon realized why this campsite had been so cheap.

Pretty sure they mean the OTHER side.

Some places don't encourage visitors.

Caution, men falling overhead.

NO NUDIES?

Open all hours (except when closed).

Seriously? Who even does this?
And when you think about it, does it even
really matter if they do?

When ET eventually went home, Elliot got a motocross bike. Chicks seemed to dig it.

Driving home a point.

Weddings, christenings and baa mitzvahs!

You have been warned!

It'll only end in tears!

Health and Safety rules gone mad!

' … darn it, Josef', said Margaret,
with a barely concealed sigh of relief,
'if only I could visit the torture chamber with you.
Alas, Health and Safety rules will not allow.'

95

Looks like this 'fast food' could take some time…